The Art of
NETWORKING

DAVID O. WOODS

The Art of NETWORKING

BEYOND THE HANDSHAKE

Published by Crowdscribed, LLC.

Edmond, Oklahoma

www.crowdscribed.com

Distributed by Lightning Source, Inc.

For ordering information or special discounts for bulk purchases, please contact

Lightning Source, Inc., at 1246 Heil Quaker Blvd, La Vergne, TN USA 37086 (615) 213-5815.

Publisher's Cataloging-In-Publication Data

(Prepared by The Donohue Group, Inc.)

Woods, David O.

  The art of networking : beyond the handshake / David O. Woods.

    p. : ill. ; cm.

    ISBN: 978-0-615-75686-8

    1. Success in business. 2. Social networks. 3. Interpersonal relations. 4. Businesspeople--Social networks. 5. Business networks. I. Title.

HF5386 .W66 2013

650.1/3

Cover design by Patrick Feehan

Interior design and composition by Christina Hicks

Edited by Callie B. Ferguson

Printed in the United States of America

13 14 15 16   10 9 8 7 6 5 4 3 2 1

First Edition

www.davidowoods.com

Table of Contents

Preface

This book is about networking. It's about deepening your business relationships. It's about the art of networking and is written in hopes of sharing the fun, relationships, and rewards that can be achieved by being awakened to well-tested networking skills.

Networking has been a key to achieving my career role as CEO of three companies, and it can help you achieve your goals too. It's just what you need to break through in today's business environment of sometimes shallow, superficial, social media-type relationships. It's a quick and entertaining read filled with simple, powerful, and memorable steps to build a network filled with rich relationships. Enjoy!

Introduction

I was twenty-three years old, fresh out of college; my blood was pumping with the excitement of the idea of working—no—"having a career" with a real business. Not that "do what you gotta do" sort of job you have during college but a real career.

I was working for a corporation that was willing to train me for six months and pay me a salary of $19,320 per year, which seemed like a lot of money in 1980, when the most money I had ever made was about $12,000 per year while I worked my way through college.

My new career was that of a factory representative for a construction equipment manufacturer. My job was to work with distributors to help them develop their markets in their respective areas of responsibility. The company had a vigorous training period, in which they had me working in the factory for about six months, spending several weeks on each production line side-by-side with some wonderfully colorful shop floor employees and going through a battery of sales and product training sessions.

Finally, I was ready for the road. Well, at least that's what they said. Truth be known, I was scared to death. Here I was, fresh out of Oklahoma State University, and put into my first territory: the New England states.

I can remember pulling up to the first distributor's location in Vermont with doubts in my head: *What kind of value can I bring to this guy? He's been in business for twenty years. What on earth can I say that would help him?*

Well, I made it through that first meeting and numerous meetings thereafter with all sorts of dealers and customers. I learned how to work hard for them and add as much value as I could. What I learned was that they needed someone to help them communicate with the factory to ensure that the factory knew what their needs were in order to sell more machines. It was a fun job, and my career seemed to be up and running. Or so I thought.

After about two years, I began to realize that just being good as a factory rep was not going to be everything I needed in my skills toolbox in order to move my career along. The first skill I knew I would need was *management*. In other words, I would need to know, and somehow demonstrate, that I knew how to manage people as well as projects. As a result, I volunteered for every project possible. I became good at learning how to take a project from ground zero and see it through to completion. It really didn't matter what the project was; every project provided an opportunity to develop plans, work within a team, and learn how to drive the implementation process. I became quite good at it and began getting "noticed," which as most corporate folks know, is one of the keys to career advancement.

The second skill I needed to learn was that of *managing and leading people,* not just projects. I learned most of my people management skills from both bad bosses as well as good bosses. I didn't have too many bad bosses, but when I did, I would watch carefully to learn what *not* to do. I realized, later in my career, that these bad examples were the most valuable management lessons I learned.

The third key area of my career development was the most elusive and difficult to grasp. From the day I started my career, people would always say, "You need to network" or "you should build your network" or something along those lines. It certainly sounded simple enough. However, no one really told me what all of that meant, nor how to do it, nor how to use it once I had it, nor the real benefit of it.

I can remember thinking, *What does networking mean? Does it mean trying to hang around with the president with the company? Having a bunch of friends? Developing a really good handshake and polishing my shoes in hopes that people will want to know me?* I was so naïve. I had no real clue how to network. It didn't help that I had been voted "shyest boy" in a high school of over 1,500 students.

So, I just started working on my own theories and thoughts about what I needed to do, combined with a lot of observation of how other successful executives networked. The first thing I began to realize was that a network was something that would very seldom have any sort of immediate benefit to my career. Instead, it would take a lot of blind faith that all the work to build the network would someday pay off. Over the next twenty-five years, I learned a lot about networking. I learned what works. I learned what doesn't work. And I learned that the art of networking goes well beyond the handshake. It shaped my career in such a way that it truly was the secret to my career, which led me to earn such positions as:

- The CEO of a company with about 1,600 employees and 140 distributors in about forty countries.

- Chairman of North American Association of Equipment Manufacturers, an association which represents all of the major manufacturers of construction, agriculture, forestry, and utility equipment.

- President of Leadership Oklahoma, an association within the state made up of about 1,200 of the state's top business, political, and education leaders.

- Founder and CEO of my own company, EXIM Group, an international business development company working with U.S. manufacturers, helping them to develop their international import and export strategies.

- Co-owner and CEO of GiANT Partners, a growth firm focused on growing companies and leaders around the world.

I'm humbled by the success I have had, and I recognize that I owe a lot of my career success to the many people who have helped and supported me along the way. However, it's important, for the sake of this book, that one recognizes the role that networking played along the way.

All of the management principles I mentioned earlier were integral to making my career a success, along with some luck, hard work, and other skills. However, each role I achieved can also be attributed to the art of networking.

Chapter One:

Let's Set the Record Straight

To understand the art of networking, the best place to start is by looking at the word *network*.

It's not Net-PLAY...

It's not Net-EAT...

It's not Net-DRINK...

It's not Net-SIT...

IT'S NET-WORK!

So many people, and many of my friends and cow-orkers over the years, feel that networking is about going to a reception and enjoying the free drinks, or piling two pounds of food onto a six-inch hors d'oeuvres plate, or sitting in a corner of a cocktail reception with friends and telling jokes.

The most valuable lesson you can learn is that the root word of networking is *work*. Most executives live inside a close network of relationships, friends, and family. It's a natural bubble that we all live in. Networking is about pushing yourself outside of the bubble. It's about intentionally building new relationships. Executives who never reach outside their relationship bubble are destined to have a career with unrealized potential.

Networking is a lifetime process. It requires constant nurturing. No matter where you are in your career—just starting or CEO of your company—the art of networking must be on the forefront of your "continuous education" agenda. For the purposes of learning the basics of how to go beyond the handshake and develop your own art of networking, I will showcase the simple yet sometimes dreaded cocktail reception and the usual corresponding business conference that so many young as well as older executives endure. We will assume, for the purposes of this book, that you're intuitive and smart enough to extrapolate the key points and apply them to a variety of circumstances in your career.

So, let's get started with our make-believe cocktail reception and conference.

Most businesspeople view a cocktail reception/conference with only a few thoughts in mind:

- What time does it start?

- What will I wear?

- Are the drinks free or will it be a cash bar?

- Will my fun friends will be there?

- Will there be food, or will I need to eat before or afterward?

- Will I meet anyone important?

All of these questions are common. However, they are also the wrong questions if you want to learn and utilize the art of networking.

To show you the key components to successful networking at a cocktail reception and conference, I'll break it down into four key elements:

- Planning

- Physical preparation

- The event itself

- The secret part: follow-up.

It's important to master each of these four areas in order to form good networking habits. Without them, you won't make lasting connections, which are the foundation of any successful business venture.

Chapter Two:

Laying the Groundwork

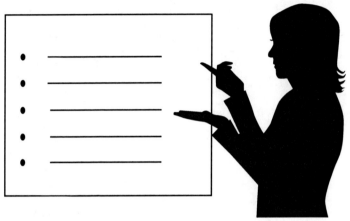

When done right, getting ready for a reception is sometimes a month-long process. Long before a reception/conference, you should find a list of who's going to be in attendance. Most reception and conference organizers provide a list of pre-registrants; however, if they don't, ask for one.

Step 1: Study the list—look for names you recognize. Look for people on the list who are somehow connected to your career now and in the future.

The Cast of Characters

Here is a sample list of networking targets:

1. Key customers, suppliers, and other closely related executives: Obviously many receptions and conferences involve a wide variety of industry-associated attendees. Learn who will be there, their titles, and their companies. Knowing your own industry clientele on a business and personal level can only improve your reputation with them.

2. Industry experts: These are people who are at the heart of your industry, which may include executives who hold positions within your industry association, executives of companies that are known as industry leaders, or trade publication editors and publishers.

3. Invited guests: Most receptions have a few invited guests outside of the normal attendee list. Learn who these people are, why they have been invited, and what impact and importance they play in your industry. Knowing the details of everyone involved can give you an edge on

your competition as well improve your web of contacts. You never know who might be attending as a guest and what opportunities he or she can present.

4. Reception/Conference managers: Knowing the people who have spent months putting together the reception conference can have immediate as well as long-term benefits. Know who they are, what their titles are, and what aspect of the reception/conference they have been involved in. They can help you locate people you want to meet at the reception, and later down the road, they can help you get in contact with conference speakers or get information on other workshops/seminars.

5. Competitors: If you don't know your competitors, look for those people on your list. Introducing yourself to your competitors is one of the classiest things you can do. It doesn't matter whether they are a new employee with your competitor's

> If possible and if applicable, get a list of invited guests that includes the names of spouses. Knowing this sort of personal information in advance can put you in the forefront of a potential contact's mind, which can only be to your advantage.

company, middle management, or the CEO, knowing your competitors on a first-name and personal basis is important. It sends the message that you're not interested in playing games or being petty. You're there to do business, and you're going to treat them with the respect you both deserve. Some of the most important relationships I had later in my career with those executives that were at one time our company's fiercest competitors.

6. Your company attendees: Many times, especially in larger companies, it's quite normal for people to work for the same company for years but not really know each other. If there are people within your company with whom you're unfamiliar or have yet to develop a relationship with, make note of them and introduce yourself, if necessary.

Step 2: Establish your target relationships—once you've studied the list, which can oftentimes be 50 to 500 people, you should begin the process of selecting four to six target relationships with whom you wish to meet and network.

Why four to six? The average reception lasts for about 45-90 minutes. Obviously, even if there were only fifty people attending the reception, it would be impossible to meet each one and have any sort of meaningful conversation. Therefore, it's critical to choose or target four to six people to seek out as part of your networking plan.

Step 3: Create the conversation—once you've selected your network targets, you should also begin developing your thought process of why you want to meet and/or network with these people. As Steve Martin said to John Candy in the classic comedy *Planes, Trains, and Automobiles*, when talking to people, "Have a point. It makes it so much more interesting to the listener!"

So what is your point? What types of things will you discuss with your network targets? Write down each of your four to six network targets' names on a piece of paper. Beside each name, begin developing your list of points, questions, comments, etc.

And Your Point Is?

So what questions should you be prepared to ask? And what actions should you plan to execute? Here are a few ideas to start the conversation:

1. Be prepared to ask a question based on something interesting that your target accomplished. This is not only flattering but also a great ice breaker that distinguishes you immediately as someone interesting, since you have obviously studied their background.

2. Plan to meet a peer in another organization for future reference or benchmarking. Competitors, similar companies, suppliers, etc., all have long-term potential networking benefits. Think about those "common areas of interest" that could be a part of some future discussion, even a few years down the road.

3. Set up a meeting. Have lunch or dinner later in the conference or sometime after the event. If you know that the one- or two-hour reception is

not long enough to accomplish some networking with your target relationships, establish a reason to meet later and further the discussion and the strength of this new person within your network.

4. Plan to discuss a key topic that is important to both of you. Many times, especially within specific industries, there are always hot topics that make for great reception fodder. Check an industry magazine or newsfeed before the reception. Have several of these types of topics that are fitting for discussion with your network targets ready.

Step 4: Refresh your memory—now that you have your list of attendees, you've selected your network targets, and you've created you list of discussion topics for each person, you're ready, right?

Review the entire list of attendees and get mental images of their faces in your head to reduce the possible embarrassment of having to read a nametag of someone whose name you should already know.

Not at all. First of all, more than likely, you have created this list several days or weeks in advance of the reception. All studies show that one's memory drops off dramatically over time, with the most dramatic loss of memory occurring within the first twenty-four hours of learning something. Therefore, one hour before the reception, review the list of attendees and your game plan again.

Step 5: Prepare for the moment—prior to the reception, make sure you have plenty of business cards. Business cards are the "currency" of good networking. Your business cards should be crisp and clean, not bent and dirty as though they've been in your wallet for the past two years. They should be made of heavy stock paper, with clean, crisp lettering. Having a nice-looking business card case is a good idea as well for these types of events. If you do keep your cards in your wallet or purse, make sure it's presentable. If your wallet or purse is dingy, tattered, or poorly organized, that sends a signal or "data point" to peo-

> Make sure your business card has all of your current information. You don't want to hand someone your card and then say, "Oh, I forgot, that phone number isn't right. Let me write down the correct one for you." Bad karma for sure!

ple that you might not want to portray. I'll discuss data points later on.

Remember that business cards are for information... your information. They should not be an advertisement for your company. Clean, simple cards are the most impressive.

Another pre-planning activity at a reception/conference is to plan a dinner for later in the conference. Although you may not know whom you will be inviting until after the reception, it's a good idea to have your dinner pre-planned. Why? Most conference hotel restaurants and surrounding restaurants (especially the good ones) tend to fill up fast. You don't want to have your best network target person agree to a dinner and then have limited options for a nice event.

Chapter Three:

Let's Get Physical

Receptions are an important place to be on your game both mentally as well as physically. Just before the reception, specifically about an hour before, is one of your most important times. It's time to prep yourself physically for the event. Many receptions occur in the evening, usually after a day of meetings or travel. Never, never, never go to a reception directly from a meeting or after arriving at the hotel. Getting yourself ready physically will have a big impact on impressions you create as well as your own mental outlook.

Prep Work

Remember that your physical appearance creates a flood of "data points" for those you meet. These data points are the small pieces of knowledge and observations people use to judge who you are and your competence. To understand data points better, let's say you're going to a fancy restaurant for dinner. You arrive, and just before you're seated, you duck into the bathroom to make sure you're looking your best. When you open the bathroom door, you see toilet paper on the floor, wet sinks, a heap of paper towels in the trashcan, and you can smell something unpleasant. You think, *If this is what the bathroom looks like, do I want to eat something from the kitchen or in the dining area? In other words, you used the data points (your observations) about the bathroom to come to a conclusion about the entire restaurant. That's the power of "data points.".*

It's the same idea in business. If you see someone at a reception with a wrinkled suit or bad breath or other unkempt attributes, this might be an indication of someone who doesn't have his or her business together either. People are looking at your data points and passing judgment about your character and competence. Ideally, of course, you should never assume anything about anyone (more on this later), but it's also important that you're not intentionally presenting any sort of unorganized aura either.

Here are ways to avoid the wrong data points:

1. **Your Breath:** Seems fairly obvious, but your breath can make or break you at a reception. Most receptions occur during the evening, and therefore it's quite possible that you've not had time (or didn't plan for it) to brush your teeth. Never attend a reception without brushing your teeth within the hour prior to the event.

2. **Look Fresh:** Even if you look in the mirror and tell yourself, "Hey, I look pretty good. I don't need a shower." Shower and shave (for men) anyway. You will look clean and crisp, and more importantly, the shower will wake up your senses so that you're 100 percent on top of your game. In fact, it has been scientifically proven that taking a shower (or at least washing your face) releases

chemicals in your brain that make you feel like you're "starting over" or refreshing your thought processes. A final check in the mirror will give you the self-confidence you need so that you can focus on your conversations without any nervousness about yourself.

3. Attire and Appearance:

Males: Your clothing should be appropriate but interesting. I've always been a tie, cufflink, and pocket square guy. I can dress up a normally dull blue blazer with a little color and conservative accessories.

Females: Don't wear anything too revealing or risqué. In fact, it's best to err on the side of formal. If a suit seems a bit overkill, wear the skirt or pants from the suit with a button-down top. Leave the open-toed shoes at home, and opt for pumps or flats. Steer clear of overly flashy jewelry.

> Whether male or female, you should be interestingly dressed, not a fashion sideshow. To err on the side of classic conservative is a safe bet.

4. **Press It:** Keeping things pressed will keep you from looking hard-pressed. Most hotel rooms have irons/ironing boards. They are there for a reason…use them! A wrinkled shirt or skirt sends a variety of signals:

> A. I don't care what I look like.
>
> B. I can't plan my day well enough to provide time to iron my clothes.
>
> C. I'm not smart enough to know that a wrinkled shirt/skirt creates a bad first impression.

5. **Properly Fitted Clothing:** Your clothes should fit well. If you don't know how to buy clothes that fit properly, or what a proper fit means, go to a higher-end department store or fine men's or women's wear store, and let an experienced clothier help you to understand the nuances of how clothing should fit.

> **Males:** You need to know the proper length of your pants, the length of your sleeves, the fit of your jacket, the proper collar size, and

other important points such as how to tie a tie and the differences between pleated pants and flat front.

F e m a l e s : Know the p r o p e r length for skirts—you don't want to wear something too short. Be sure to

> Later in my career, I actually used a private clothier who came to my home. He would look through my clothes and help me pick the right mix of slacks, jackets, suits, ties, and shoes to give me the greatest flexibility but with the highest quality. I was amazed at how long these classic clothes would last. It's true: You get what you pay for.

have trousers fitted while wearing pumps so that the hem falls at the right length. Make sure your suits are properly fitted, and have a selection for both winter and summer.

6. **Shine Your Shoes:** It may seem old school, but many people still judge a person by the shine on their shoes. This goes for both males and females: The

> Only wear leather-soled shoes to a reception. Rubber-soled shoes may be great for walking, but they have no place in a business reception.

image you portray with your shoes is similar to the difference between wrinkled or pressed shirts. Make sure you know how to put a shine on your shoes.

7. **Fingernails:**

> **Males:** Your nails should be neatly trimmed and clean.

> **Females:** Make sure your nails are trimmed and clean, and avoid neon or flashy nail polish. If you're wearing fake nails, make sure they're not so long as to get in the way of everyday activities.

8. **Hair:** Make sure your hair is well groomed, recently cut, combed, and in place. Again, it's like the wrinkled shirt story. Don't be unprepared.

Remember, your physical appearance is one of the only things your network target has in his/her arsenal to evaluate who and what kind of person you are. "Looking the part helps you get the chance to fill it!"

Etiquette

Before you begin your world of networking, crack a book or two on behavior and etiquette. To some, this may seem antiquated, but having proper form at a dinner reception can make or break someone's impression of you. Being from the Midwest myself, some people balk at what they might call "city etiquette." They have their own familiar country ways of doing things. They say, "I just wasn't brought up that way." Well, just because you weren't brought up that way doesn't mean you shouldn't act like it. When you refuse to learn proper etiquette, it puts a barrier between you and your potential success.

My father was a career military man, retiring after thirty-three years as a two-star general in the U.S. Air Force. Growing up in this environment came with a certain level of grooming that I felt at the time was overdone. In retrospect I now understand why my parents were so adamant about etiquette.

I can remember one time telling my father, "People really don't care that much about manners and etiquette," and I have remembered for years the words he then said: "Etiquette matters to those who know good etiquette. They may not say anything, but they notice."

Today, I know how true that is. As a CEO, I've promoted many individuals with the highest skill sets, including social skills. As I have said to many college students during my lectures, "Etiquette is important. Get over it, and learn it." If you're unsure of the many rules, manners, and nuances of proper etiquette, visit your local bookstore or go online. There are numerous books and websites on the topic, all with valuable information.

To fully appreciate the rules of etiquette, one must understand that at its core, each rule of etiquette has its formation as a way of showing respect to others. Therefore, when you don't use or understand the rules of etiquette, you're showing others that you do not respect them.

For example, the reason it's important to know how to properly "close" your plate (the act of laying your utensils across the middle of the plate when you're finished eating) is to alert the waiter that it's okay to take your plate away without the waiter needing to interrupt your conversation.

Stay on Target

During a reception in which you have properly prepared, remember why you're there, and especially remember these two rules:

- **Eating is not the purpose:** I eat very little at most receptions. My goal is to stay focused on the people, not the food. Also, food can be extremely awkward, allowing the chance for crumbs to fall on your clothing or on your chin. It's a high-risk activity that can easily be avoided. Typically, I only eat if I've made contact with one of my targeted key relationships and they want to eat.

- **Drinking is not the purpose:** Certainly, you're free to have a drink (with or without alcohol); however, if you are drinking alcohol, be aware of your body's limits. You don't want to embarrass yourself by ingesting too much of what my father used to call "blabber juice." Which obviously points to the tendency of people talking too much after a few drinks.

> Another aspect of drinking is *what* you drink. You want to make sure you are in synch with your network targets. If they are wine or scotch drinkers, don't drink Bud from a bottle. Learn to broaden your palate so that you can adapt to each unique situation. Even in a beer environment, I would recommend drinking beer from a glass. Bottles are for college students, not businesspeople.

Keep yourself aligned with your purpose for being at a reception, and you'll find it much easier to focus on your target relationships and having meaningful conversation with them. If you're not fussing with a drink or filling up on free food, you'll be sure to leave with the information you need to create an expanded network.

Chapter Four:

The Main Event

Finally, you're in full swing at the reception. You've identified your network targets, you've developed your list of conversation points for each person, and you've prepared yourself physically. You're on your game!

Nametag Etiquette

Usually when entering a reception, you're given a nametag (or you've received it earlier). Nametags are usually one of the more misunderstood accessories of a reception and conference.

First, let's make it clear: Nametags are not intended to be a fashion statement. They are not to be worn attached to your purse, nor your belt. A nametag has but one purpose: to inform the other person of your name. Therefore, it should be easy to see on your body and legible. At some receptions you are required to write your own name on the nametag. Make sure you write it as large and as legible as possible.

Nametags should be positioned in the appropriate location on your body. Many people often put nametags on the left side of their body, attached to a pocket, but this is not the best place. Nametags should be worn on the right side of your body, as close to the top of your chest as possible. This position allows the other person to first focus on your hand during a handshake, and then, his/her eyes will naturally move up along your right hand, past the right side of your chest, and toward your eyes to say, "Hello." You want the path of their eyes to easily cross over your nametag.

If you wear your nametag on the left side of your body, or on your belt, or on your purse, the other person will need to be somewhat of a contortionist in order to see your name, because they'll be looking at your right hand, then leaning over to see the left side of your body, and then up to your eyes. The most awkward and uncomfortable feeling is seeing someone you should know and needing to read their nametag in order to remember their name. Your goal is to make the other person avoid this potential embarrassment by providing your name in the most obvious location possible.

Positioning

When you walk into the reception area, the first thing to do is adjust your position and your stance. You want to stand in a high-traffic area—such as near the entrance but not *too* close. You don't want to bombard people as they come in. One option is to stand near the bar area, since everyone will likely be heading that direction once they walk in. But don't block the bar area while chatting, as it's perceived as poor etiquette. Another good place is near the buffet line—but not *in* the buffet line. As people wait in line to fill their plates, stand just to the side of the line until you have the opportunity to engage your target relationship in conversation.

Your position is important at the conference as well. During any sit-down portions of a conference, you should sit close to the front, putting yourself directly in the line of sight toward the speaker. Even though you're not speaking, when others are staring at you from behind, they see your mannerisms, notice your clothing, and generally feel like they know you, even though you might never have introduced yourself. It's an undercover way to get noticed. A nice side benefit to sitting near the front is that speakers are always more interesting when you're closer to them.

Back to the Reception...

Once you're in position, you're ready to start introducing yourself and getting down to business. Remember these five important points:

1. **The Hand Shake:** Although it's a well-known fact that a hand-shake should be firm, it still amazes me how many people still don't seem to know it. A handshake should be the physical extension of your vocal "hello." It should be warm and inviting. Handshakes are not a test of strength. Do not try to outsqueeze the other person. Instead, let your hand do your talking to tell the person, "I'm a warm and friendly person who is genuinely happy to meet you." Putting lotion on your hands prior to a reception adds to the warmth of your handshake.

> Holding a drink can cause major problems for the process of a handshake. Your drink should always be in your left hand. Why? Well, obviously, handshakes are done with the right hand. However, the more important reason to keep your drink in your left hand the entire duration of the reception is so that your right hand doesn't get wet and clammy. It's virtually impossible, and not a very attractive gyration, to try to dry your hand on your slacks or dress in order to prep for a handshake. You want your right hand to stay warm and inviting.

2. **Eye Contact:** During the earlier days in my career, I was once in charge of planning and organizing a reception/conference for our com-

pany and our dealers. It was a big responsibility. During the first night of the reception, I found myself scanning the room looking for problems and issues. While standing in the reception, I ended up chatting with one of our dealers (who was also a good friend of mine). As he tried to talk

> If you ever watch a good interviewer on television, you'll notice that he or she always keeps his or her eyes locked onto the eyes of the person being interviewed. Polished and professional interviewers seem to stare right through the eyes of their subjects, which tells them, "Every word you say is important to me." Your eye contact with your network targets should be of the same intensity.

to me, my eyes wandered across the room, checking things out, looking to see who was there and who wasn't. Additionally, I didn't face this dealer; instead, I turned slightly to the side so that I could have a better view of the room. After about two minutes of this drill, my friend sort of "got in my face" and said, "You know, if I'm boring you or there's someone more important you need to chat with, you can leave." Although he said it tongue-in-cheek (luckily we really were good friends), it sent an everlasting memory into my brain about the importance of eye contact.

3. **Forward-Facing Stance:** As I mentioned above with my story about my friend, I also turned slightly to the side and was not facing him directly. This is known as "leaking out of the conversation." It's a classic and incorrect stance to be angled slightly away from the person with whom you're talking. Leaking tells the other person that you're bored and that you're already positioning yourself for a quick getaway as soon as someone more interesting comes along. The proper stance should be directly facing the other person. Your feet should be firmly planted. Just like your eyes, your stance should tell the other person that he is the most important person on the face of the earth, and nothing is going to distract you from your conversation.

4. **Voice inflection:** How you sound is another physical aspect of the reception. The goal is to be yourself, not someone else. Don't take on a used-car salesman approach as though you're everyone's best buddy, talking loudly and putting

on airs. On the other hand, don't be boring. Be loud enough to be heard by your target, and be as inviting as possible in your speech.

5. **Smile:** The best tactic to ensure your voice reflects your true inner warmth is to smile. When you smile, it's impossible to be boring. People love to be with a fun person. Practice learning to smile, even if it's initially a little awkward to smile to yourself. People will be attracted to you in ways you cannot imagine because you will be approachable, fun, and friendly. You can try it as an experiment at your next reception. Try keeping a neutral face or even a frown for just five minutes, and see who comes over to you to talk. But then try smiling for five minutes. Not a goofy smile, just something pleasant. You'll find more people wanting to speak with you when you look easily accessible.

Time Management

Now that you're inside the reception, you need to follow some basic steps to maximize your limited amount of time and locate your network targets. There are several tactics to employ to find your network targets:

- **Have a slight sense of urgency:** This may seem odd, but if you portray a sense of urgency and begin asking people, "Have you seen _____?" Others will assume you have something very important to discuss with that person, and they will, in turn, begin to help you locate your network targets. Better yet, some of them will actually find your network targets for you and will tell them that you are looking for them. What better way to begin creating an image that you have something important to say? In many cases your network targets will begin looking for you, and/or when you meet, they will be anticipating your words.

- **Use friends and business associates:** Make sure these people know that you're on a mission. They can help you find and identify your network targets. This is especially helpful if you've never actually met the person and do not know what they look like.

- **Use conference personnel:** The people who organize a reception/conference can be your most valuable asset for networking purposes. I always befriend these people. Well before the conference, I will usually e-mail them to ask for the list of attendees. During this interaction I will always offer to help them in any way I can. For example, oftentimes, someone will not show up for an assigned task such as providing an invocation prior to a dinner. I usually use this example as something I could do should they get in a bind. They will rarely need you; however, they will always be appreciative of your thoughtfulness. Once you become friends with conference personnel, they will gladly help you find and identify your network targets.

- **Stand in high-traffic areas:** As was mentioned earlier, if your network targets have not yet arrived, your next tactic is to maximize the moment. And the best way to meet new people is to be seen. Remember, standing somewhere near the bar or the entrance to the reception is an excellent way to meet new people. Also, this will allow you the visibility you need to spot your network targets as they enter the room.

Capturing Your Target Relationship's Attention

To capture and hold your target relationships, utilize the following tactics:

- If the event is a cash bar, buy your target relationship a drink. When you're busy buying a target relationship a drink, what do you think they're going to be doing? Waiting for you! Once you've "invested" time and effort in them, they will want to stay with you as a gesture to say, "Thanks for the drink."

- If it's a free bar, offer to go get a drink for your network target by saying, "I want to chat with you." By utilizing this tactic, your network target will, again, stay in place and wait patiently for your return. And, similar to the tactic for the cash bar, your target will want to spend time with you in thanks for your efforts.

- If the reception has a program in which you will be seated, invite your network target to sit with you. Most people don't "pre-plan" whom they will be sitting next to, so your offer to sit with them is a wonderfully non-threatening way to get to know them. This tactic can work with the conference as well. Offering to sit next to someone during a conference can create a shared experience, which is key to establishing a relationship with a target relationship.

How to Listen

Now that you have successfully located your target relationship and you have their attention, you're now ready to employ the most important skill you have: listening. Listening is the key to creating a quick yet lasting impression. It's also the key to the necessary follow-up you will do later to cultivate your newest member of your personal network. Listening is not hard if you will focus on three key areas:

- Listen for "nuggets of commonality." No matter whom you're talking to, it's always possible to find areas of common interest and/or background.

- Utilize a series of questions (pre-planned if necessary) that will quickly show the other person that you are truly interested in them. This process will allow you to find those nuggets of commonality. Try phrases like, "Tell me about what you do." "What's the best part about your job?" "Tell me about your company."

- Focus on the areas of fascination. Although you will find several "nuggets of commonality," try to focus on those areas that have the most potential for fascinating conversation. If you have the choice between talking about his/her book they just wrote, choose that topic over the fact you were both a few minutes late due to traffic.

If you can start the conversation by just listening to the other person speak for a while, you can learn much about the person without having to ask many questions. When you give people that courtesy, they will return it, and pretty soon you'll be sharing about *your* job, *your* company, and *your* interests.

The Loner

After all of your preparation, and all of your hard work to get prepared for the reception/conference, it won't always go the way you anticipate. Therefore you need to adopt my favorite tactic, which is, "Don't let the plan get in the way of an opportunity." And those opportunities really aren't that hard to find.

For example, if you've ever been to a dinner reception and conference, you've probably seen "the loner." The loner is the person who has heaped his or her plate full of food and is sitting at table at the back of the room all alone. Many people see this as a lost cause or a dead end. This is not necessarily the case.

Most of the time, someone sitting alone with a plate of food doesn't indicate a poor business contact; it just indicates that person is not comfortable in the reception/conference scenario. Don't ignore them. Approach them directly and be friendly. Listen to them, find common interests, and be confident in your posture and approach. Chances are, you'll probably become a hero for coming over and rescuing him or her from an uncomfortable situation. You might even make an important connection. Some of the most important relationships I have are with people whom others perceive as loners.

Working Tables of Eight

Conference dinners can actually reduce your ability to network unless you know a few tricks. Imagine this situation: At dinner, you're sitting at one of those awkward eight-person tables, and you can barely hear anything from the person across from you. It's hard to get a conversation started. What should you do?

First, when you approach your eight-person table, don't sit down. Instead, stand up and take the lead. Engage someone to your right or left and get to know them briefly. You'll have more time to talk with them after you sit down.

Once you've learned a little bit about the person immediately next to you, make your way around the table and introduce yourself to everyone. This process of "opening the table" is an easy way to break the ice at the table and get everyone comfortable enough to chat. Once you've met everyone and taken a seat, engage the person directly across from you and say, "I'm really interested to hear about your company. Tell me about that." In this way, you've engaged everyone at the table, and you've started the conversation for everyone.

Chapter Five:

The Best-Kept Secret?
Follow-Up

Probably the most overlooked yet most important aspect to networking is following up. It's the best way to show a potential client or new relationship that he or she is important and worth making a connection with. So how does the modern businessperson follow up? Here another secret: It starts *during* the reception/conference.

Put Down the Gun

Once you've made contact and had a positive conversation with someone at the cocktail or dinner reception, go online and look them up. Check their company's profile; their role in the company; their interests, if possible. Then, the next day at the conference, seek them out. Be welcoming, and ask them to sit with you for a workshop or speaker session. Bring up their interests and background if you want. What you're looking to do is start the conversation and have a shared experience. This shared experience is a subtle bond that could lead to even more important discussions.

Remember that you're not at a conference or a reception to make a sale, or to do a deal, or to ask for something. Your purpose is to cultivate a relationship.

It's Not About You

Remember this simple quote about networking, and you'll have a better idea how to approach your target relationships: "Networking is farming, not hunting. Put down the gun." Oftentimes when businesspeople attend conferences and receptions, they're only thinking about one person: themselves. *I've* got to meet the speaker; *I* need to make sure *I* get approached by someone important; *I* hope *I* get wined and dined by someone this evening. But let me challenge you to rethink this. If you're only thinking and worrying about you, you're probably going to miss out an on opportunity to connect with someone important who might otherwise have flown under your radar.

There are many ways to make a new contact feel welcomed and appreciated, and it can be as simple as a handwritten note or as impactful as a personal-ized gift. For example, say you've been studying that list of conference attendees during your planning phase, and you run across a name on the list that you've seen before. Maybe you've met them before at another conference, or maybe you've never met them but have been meaning to make contact. Capitalize on this opportunity to make a connection. When you get to the hotel, have a handwritten note left at the front desk for them when they check in. If you received a handwritten note from a desk clerk at hotel from someone you met at a conference, you'd certainly feel like a VIP.

If you're not much of a letter writer, try having a nice basket of food or maybe a bottle of wine left on their bed when they check in. You'd be surprised how much of an impression a small gift basket makes.

Let's say you're at the reception, and there's a constant stream of people you need to talk with. You see that you're not going to have time for that one person you really meant to talk with. Rather than let that opportunity pass you by, stop by the bar and have their favorite drink delivered over to them. That sends the signal that they haven't been overlooked and are still important to you.

Even when a key relationship isn't at the same conference you are, you can still be thinking about them.

If a speaker at a conference you're attending is signing copies of his or her book, and you think a key relationship might find it interesting, buy two copies—one for you and one for a friend—and have the speaker sign them. Sending an autographed copy of a book is a great way to show others that you know their interests and want to stay connected.

Personalize It

If you go the personal gift route, you don't have to buy something expensive, but you do have to put in some thought and make the gift personal in some way. Start by just sending a card, and not just a birthday or Christmas card. Step it up and think creatively. Try sending a Thanksgiving or Halloween card, anything that stands out. If you send a Christmas or birthday card, it's going to arrive in a stack of cards from hundreds of others, and you won't be remembered. Making a statement that's unusual but friendly is the best way to make an imprint.

Here's a true story about an inexpensive gift that went a long way: One year, I was traveling by myself on business in China. I stopped in a marketplace for some souvenirs for myself and my family, when I saw a very unusual object. It looked to me like a hugely oversized man's shaving brush. As soon as I saw it, I thought of one of my network relationships who collects shaving brushes. In fact, he has somewhere around 200 of them. When I saw this giant brush, I immediately thought, *What a great gift idea. He'll probably think it's funny.* I picked it up for $5.

Later on, when I returned home, I discovered that it was actually a calligraphy brush, not meant for shaving, but when I gave it to my friend, you would have thought that I had given him his third child! He positively loved it, and it definitely improved our business relationship. Because I was thinking not only of myself but also business connections, I was able to pick up this gift and make a distinct impression.

If you're not sure about your network target's interests or hobbies, try something a bit more general. Say you and a target went to a golf tournament, and you took a couple of pictures together out on the fairway. If you just e-mail a photo or send a print to your new friend, you might be remembered for a moment, but in the long run, that photo is going to end up in a random folder or drawer without another thought. The way to really impress and personalize the gift is to put that photo into a frame. If a key relationship receives a picture of the two of you in a nice frame with maybe a nameplate on the bottom, that picture is sure to go on a shelf, somewhere it will be seen and leave a lasting impression.

A Memorable Dinner

In today's world, everyone eats out on a regular basis. It's no longer a luxury or even memorable to eat at a restaurant. However, it is possible to create a very memorable dinner for a prospective client or target. Here are the steps and the formula:

- **The Restaurant:** Choose a higher-end restaurant that will understand the nuances of a special evening. Steer clear of commercialized chains and select instead a local chef whom you can trust to provide a unique experience.

- **The Maître 'D:** Go early and speak with the maître 'd. Tell him or her that you want to host a client, and ask what can be done to make this an incredible evening.

- **The Table:** Ask for "the best seat in the house." The maître 'd knows exactly where in the restaurant it will be and will gladly seat you there.

- **The Waiter:** Ask the maître 'd who the best waiter or waitress is and then ask to meet him or her. Let the server know that the dinner is very special, and you're looking to him or her for ideas of how to make it truly memorable. Let the server know that you'll add a 25 percent tip to the bill in exchange for his or her help.

- **The Drinks:** Let the waiter know what drinks you want upon arrival. It will impress your guest if his or her favorite drink arrives without asking.

- **The Chef:** Ask to meet the chef. He will usually gladly spend a few minutes with you. Tell the chef that you want him to enjoy preparing the meal as much you will enjoy eating it. You can even suggest the chef to create whatever he wants, even if it's not on the menu. Or you can set the budget for the meal. I usually say, "Have fun and be creative, but shoot for a target of $75 per plate." You'll be amazed at how often you get a lot more than $75 of creative value from a professional chef. Finally, invite the chef to come and visit your table during the meal and explain how he prepared a special item or sauce.

- **The Check:** Pre-sign a credit card form and add the 25 percent to ensure a bill never shows up.

In other words, tell the restaurant what you need and your available budget, and then let them take over creatively. Once you hand over the creative reigns, you'll be surprised what can happen. Maybe you'll have your own personal waiter throughout the meal, or maybe a signature dish can be prepared especially for you and your target. It will leave a very memorable impression.

Letter Writing

In our technology-driven society, the art of letter writing has become a bit of a mystery to some businesses executives. Most businesspeople communicate via e-mail or text message, and it's a pretty quick-and-dirty exchange with not a lot of thought put in. If you really want to give a put-together impression for a potential client or network relationship, break out the old pen and paper and write them a letter. And not just a few lines of text will do; make it a page long, with a nice header and a good signature at the bottom. If you're not sure about how to write a letter of this length, there are all kinds of web tutorials and books available to help you succeed.

As an example of a good occasion to write a letter, say a client or target relationship of yours has won an award of some kind. Write that person a congratulatory note. Write the letter in a way that shows you're bragging on their company as much as the person. In other words, write a letter they can share with others. And once you've finished, find a nice frame for it. Remember that a framed note is sure to end up in a visible area and not in a drawer!

Chapter Six:

No Filtering

In this last chapter, I'm going to relate maybe the most important thing people overlook when making connections at an event: filtering. Now, when I say that, most people think of being careful about what you say, and although you should do that, that's not what I mean. Too many businesspeople make the mistake of "filtering relationships" too quickly, meaning they often *assume* something about a potential business contact right away, often based solely on their appearance, without actually talking to them or relating to them somehow.

Remember the loner? Because others were too busy "filtering" him or her out of their sights, the loner went unnoticed and left out. But because you weren't trolling the floor for someone who "looked" like they would be a good contact and instead took the time to introduce yourself to someone others ignored, you walked away with an important connection.

Here's my personal true story about how not filtering relationships too early can help you: One year, there was a conference coming to my city in which international consulates from around the world were attending. The conference personnel had the task of pairing up business executives with different consulates to show them around the area, give them a warm reception, and provide them with a dinner before the actual conference. The conference personnel were inundated with requests from executives to be paired with specific consulates such as those from the more popular countries of China, Japan, England, Germany, etc. However, the conference had a few consulates from some lesser-known countries that were very difficult to place, making their job very difficult.

Rather than adding to the confusion, I called up the conference managers and asked, "Which consulates are you having trouble pairing? Who do you need me to take care of? I'm sure there's probably one consulate you just can't get seem to match up, right? Who is it? I'll take him."

The conference manager who answered responded, "God bless you! I have just the person for you. We can't find anyone to take him. He's the ambassador from Turkmenistan, and he's brought his wife and twelve-year-old daughter with him."

I gladly agreed and began planning for the evening. Normally, this kind of reception would be just the two of us at a nice restaurant discussing business. But because I wanted to make this a truly memorable evening for this man, and since no one else seemed to want to take him on, I decided to do something different. I called up the ambassador and told him that we'd be having a quiet dinner at my home with my family, and he could bring his wife and daughter with him. Our children could play together in our pool while we ate and talked. We made it very simple; we set up a nice table in the backyard by the pool, lit candles, and had a nice meal catered in.

When the ambassador and his family arrived, everything went very smoothly. In fact, I learned quite a bit that evening. Unbeknownst to me at the time, an ambassador is a much higher position than consulate, and I had volunteered myself to entertain the highest-ranking official attending our conference. The fact that I refrained from filtering out someone who *seemed* unimportant led me to the ambassador of Turkmenistan. As it turns out, Turkmenistan contains the world's fourth largest reserve of natural gas, and at that time, I had a client who was in the oil and gas business. We were able to make some very important connections because of that simple backyard dinner. Even our children kept in touch over the next year or so, and it ended up being an incredibly positive experience for both of us.

Though this story is a bit extravagant when it comes to filtering, and most of the time you're not going to be dining with an ambassador of a foreign country as a result, there's still an important lesson to be learned here. Assuming anything about anyone without having introduced yourself and learning more about that person can only bring you missed opportunities. Don't overlook anyone.

Sometimes an opportunity or connection is hidden beneath a scruffy shoe or a wrinkled suit. Sometimes it's not. But you can't let your assumptions dictate your actions. That's why you have to be the example in the room. You have to be the person with impeccable grooming, good etiquette, strong listening skills, a welcoming demeanor, and excellent follow-up skills to leave an impression upon the others who might be assuming something about *you*. Don't let someone assume you're not a perfect specimen of a business contact.

Afterword

If you're utilizing all of your newfound networking skills correctly, be prepared for the multitude of connections and opportunities that will come your way. It takes some practice to overcome nerves or an introvert personality, but even just trying one or two of the techniques I've outlined can only help you in your desire to develop business connections. As you try tactics like opening a table, buying a unique gift, planning a memorable dinner, or just becoming more engaged as a listener, you'll find that you can compile these different skills to suit any situation. And now you don't have to learn each of these valuable tactics piecemeal, as I did. You can learn the skills I developed over the course of my career in one place. It's made an immeasurable difference in my career and personal life. In fact, mastering the art of networking will not only bring business but also new and lifelong relationships for you too. Enjoy!

Notes:

Notes:

Notes:

Notes:

Notes:

Notes: